MARTIN LUTHER

Reformer Or Heretic?

BY THOMAS E. PATTEN

C.S.S Publishing Co., Inc.
Lima, Ohio

MARTIN LUTHER: Reformer Or Heretic?

Copyright © 1992 by
The C.S.S. Publishing Company, Inc.
Lima, Ohio

Second Printing 1992

All rights reserved. No part of this publication may be reproduced, stored in a retrieval system, or transmitted in any form or by any means, electronic, mechanical, photocopying, recording, or otherwise, without the prior permission of the publisher. Inquiries should be addressed to: The C.S.S. Publishing Company, Inc., 628 South Main Street, Lima, Ohio 45804.

Scripture quotations are from the *Revised Standard Version of the Bible,* copyrighted 1946, 1952 (c), 1971, 1973, by the Division of Christian Education of the National Council of the Churches of Christ in the USA. Used by permission.

9220 / ISBN 1-55673-407-7   PRINTED IN U.S.A.

Lovingly to my wife Brenda who has enriched my life and supported my work in all endeavors. Since we have been justified through faith we have peace with God through our Lord Jesus Christ.

(Romans 5:1)

Table Of Contents

Introduction 7

Part 1
   The Early Years 11
   Discussion Questions 21

Part 2
   Controversy With Rome And
      The Diet Of Worms 25
   Discussion Questions 34

Part 3
   Luther's Legacy — The Later Years 37
   Discussion Questions 44

Works Cited 45

Martin Luther: Reformer Or Heretic?

INTRODUCTION

On October 31, 1517, there was only one Protestant — Martin Luther. A few years later, there were millions. The violent explosion known as the Reformation split the church of the 16th century into a number of segments, of which the Lutheran Church is one.

This book arises from my conviction that there is a need for a concise and discerning study about Martin Luther. This intense reformer faced fierce struggles and ultimately the utter disdain of his father when he chose to turn his life to God. However, the monastery was at first only to add to young Martin's confusion. He pondered agonizingly to understand the surety of God's grace and forgiveness.

Luther had been a Roman Catholic priest who loved the church and had no intention of separating from it. But he ventured to protest in 1517 against some of the church's doctrines such as the sale of certificates known as indulgences which was said to reduce the time a soul must stay in purgatory. His actions led to a confrontation at the Trial at Worms. The end result was a break with the Roman Catholic Church that soon was beyond repair.

The concluding section will bear witness to how many of Martin Luther's concepts are alive and quite active in contemporary Christian communities. At the end of each section in the book is a list of discussion questions, which should aid in understanding the complex man that was Martin Luther, as well as theological issues in the community asked by members and non-members alike.

Ludher ex Mansfeld" matriculated in the faculty of Arts, at the University of Erfurt. Erfurt was a renowned university, one of the oldest (1397) and best attended in Germany, and known as a center of International Study *(stadium generale)*. At this time its faculty of Law was notable, and Luther may have gone there rather than to Leipzig because he was destined for the law, his parents were sure of that.

Luther had bed and board at the student hostel of St. George, and made many friends. Young Luther talked a good deal (they nicknamed him 'the philosopher') and learned to play the lute. He took the usual arts courses and proceeded to the bachelor's degree in 1502. At the age of 22, Luther took his master's degree and placed second among 17 candidates. In an age when only a small proportion of those who went up proceeded as far as the master's degree, Luther had done all that his parents could have hoped.

For a youth in his position, having respect to the resources and station of his parents, there were two possibilities — lawyer or priest. It may be that the sturdy anti-clericalism which Hans Luther shared with many of his class and age was decisive. Anyway, Hans Luther paid for a new copy of the *Corpus Juris* and Martin Luther entered in the faculty of law. He might one day make a name for himself in Saxony as a public notary of Eisleben or Eisenach, or he might achieve the dignity of an official at the Court of the Elector Frederick.

Suddenly all these thoughts were thrown into chaos. To his dismay and rage, Hans Luther learned that the son, for whom he hoped so much, who had but recently been home, talking about his music and his literary friends, had decided to enter religion and was seeking admission to the monastery of the Austin Friars in Erfurt.

Various reasons have been presented for the sudden decision of Luther to become a monk. The real cause, I believe, lay in a torturing sense of sin and a longing for reconciliation with God, experienced by many deeply spiritual Christians at one time or another in their lives. The cloister had been the refuge of such persons for a thousand years and to it the Saxon student naturally was drawn to find rest for his soul.

After all, the seemingly abrupt vow is only the natural culmination of previous experiences. The strict disciple of a stern and pious home, the priestly circle of friends at Eisenach, had all pointed the boy to a career then regarded as the perfection of Christianity.

The influences in the same direction at Erfurt were also very strong. This flourishing, but by no means large town, boasted 20 cloisters, 23 churches, 36 chapels, in all more than 100 buildings devoted to religious uses. Among the numerous orders represented by Chapters at "Little Rome," as the devout city was called, the strongest were those of the begging friars, the Franciscans, Dominicans and Augustinians.

In September 1505, Martin Luther received the tonsure (the shaving of the hair on the head) and took the cowl (hooded garment). As a clerical novice he was taught all the prescribed acts of reverence: how and when and before whom to bend the knee or throw himself prostrate on the ground; to go about with eyes downcast; to do the various nominal chores, for example, scrubbing floors, and helping in the kitchen; to keep up a happy pretense of humility; even to go through the motions of begging bread in the street.

His whole life was ordered strictly and completely by his preceptor. Great stress was laid on confession and on the reading and study of the Bible. He enjoyed a single cell, nine feet by six, in which were one chair, one table, one candlestick and a straw bed. He had no heat in his cell, a very severe discipline during a German winter. He ate twice a day only, once a day on fast days (of which there were some hundred in the year).

In September 1506, one year after taking the cowl, Luther professed the vows of poverty, chastity and obedience, and proceeded through the orders of sub-deacon, deacon and priest. When, on May 2 the following year, he was ordained priest in the Cathedral at Erfurt, his father was invited to the ceremony, and though he appeared with a fine company of some 50 horses and gave a handsome gift to the monastery, even at that late stage he openly showed his disapproval of his son's self-chosen career.

After his ordination Luther was not to work in silence for the perfection of his soul, but was to resume studies in the school connected with the monastery. This proved to be the pattern of his life. Martin Luther was born to preach and teach. Fortunately his spiritual mentors saw this and gave him the opportunity to study and work. This will always stand to their credit. He applied himself with such zeal and success that 18 months after his first mass, he was called to the recently founded University of Wittenberg to teach Aristotle's Ethics. He spent a year in this position, at the same time continuing his own studies. In the fall of 1509, Luther was sent back to Erfurt "because he had not satisfied the Wittenberg Faculty." This sentence in the Dean's book, with Luther's own later addition, "because he had no means: — Erfurt must pay," is usually taken to mean that he had no money to pay the academic fees. It is also probable that there was some trouble about the lectures he was to give; he wished to discontinue philosophy and take up the Bible. It was the academic rule that before lecturing on the Scriptures a young professor should devote three semesters to expounding Peter Lombard's Sentences, the common textbook in theology. This Luther did at Erfurt, where he remained for about 21 months, until he was called back to a permanent position at Wittenberg in the summer of 1511. This stay at Erfurt was interrupted by the journey to Rome.

Such is the bare history of the outward events of the seven years in the cloister. Far more interesting is the record of his inward life during the same period. Instead of finding peace within the monastic cell, his doubt and despair only increased. His table-talk, taken down late in life, is full of statements of the utter depth of the suffering of the doubter of his own salvation. God appeared to him as a cruel judge: he felt that he could never do enough to win God's favor and deserve free pardon. Though there is some reason to believe that in looking back he painted his past even darker than it really was, there can be no doubt that he went through agonies before he attained strength and peace of mind.

Sometime between 1512-15, he went to Rome on business connected with his Order, and was affronted at the cynical professionalism of the clergy and the worldliness in high places. In 1512, encouraged by his teacher and friend, John Staupitz, he took his Doctor of Divinity, a status which involved defending sacred truths in public. On the retirement of Staupitz, Luther succeeded him as a professor of biblical theology. He now became involved in a university turmoil which was European-wide, the tension between an older scholasticism and the new humanism based on a return to "the Bible and the Old Feathers." This involved Luther in growing antagonism to his old teachers, especially the Nominalists at Erfurt. Alongside university lectures, which were apt to be dull, the regular debates provided a useful ground for airing new and controversial opinions. In Wittenberg they took place on Fridays at the promotion of students. Luther presided over many of these debates when he was dean, and one occasion in April 1517 gave rise to a formidable series of 97 theses which were an all-out attack on the schoolmen, and especially the Nominalist tradition of Gabriel Biel and of Luther's own teachers, Trutvetter and Usingen.

Martin Luther had by this time something of a reputation for controversy, and his correspondence reflects the fact that he had seriously annoyed the Erfurt theologians. Luther wanted his 97 theses debated, and offered to go to Erfurt himself to defend his propositions in the university or in the monastery. It may have been the most carefully planned act of public defiance of Luther's career, and it seems to have misfired completely.

By the autumn of 1517, Luther had come a long way. We misunderstand entirely if we think of him as a restless innovator, or, in Gerhard Ritter's fine phrase, as a kind of academic bully. But Luther's fight was within his conscience, and it was in the city of Mansoul he learned the art of the warfare he would one day employ. His anger against the Nominalist teachings, and the Aristotelian domination of the schools, was that they were leading souls astray, deceiving men with a false sense of security which failed them, as Luther had seen again and again, when they stood terrified by the face of death. But conscience for Luther meant facing the wrath of God, rather than preoccupation with his own emotions, and so led directly to the great saving objectives of his Theology of the Cross.

It is true that a culture was dying, and that much of the life of the church was entangled with it. But what was dying, like the Holy Roman Empire, and what had the secret renewal, like the Papacy, was not easy to discern. A strange world was being born, its birth pangs were a series of political and social tensions which baffled statesmen, while for one new world across the Atlantic to attract the bodies of men, a dozen new horizons of the mind were opening, offering the church that challenge to baptize a culture which in the first, the fifth and the ninth centuries she had marvelously accepted, but which now, sick, enfeebled and in sin, she was unable to comprehend. Over the whole doctrine of the church, of papal authority, the Doctrine of Merit, the Doctrine of Indulgences, there reigned an uncertainty and vagueness which was regarded as a prime cause of the Reformation, and not least of the hesitant attitude of the orthodox with regard to Luther's teachings.

The Indulgence was primarily the commutation of the act of satisfaction which was one of the three parts of the Sacrament of Penance (contrition; confession; satisfaction). In 1300, Boniface VIII issued a Jubilee Indulgence to all who visited the tombs of the Apostles on 15 successive days: originally limited to 100-year intervals, the Jubilee became more and more frequent as papal financial difficulties deepened. The practice found theoretical justification in the Doctrine of the Treasurer of Merits of Christ and the Saints, expounded by Alexander of Hales *(Summa, VI, qu, 83)* and confirmed by the Bull Unigenitus of Clement VI, 1343, which includes the statement that Christ "acquired a treasure for the Church Militant." In 1467 Pope Sixtus IV extended the scope of an Indulgence to the souls in purgatory. By the beginning of the 16th century, Indulgences had become a holy business *(sacrum negotium)* so complex as to demand the superintendence of the Banking House of Fugger.

In 1514, young Hohenzollern Prince Albert of Brandenburg, (age 23) became the Archbishop of Mainz and the Primacy of Germany. Enormous fees were due to the Pope for his accumulation of benefices, and Albert was soon heavily in debt to the accommodating but watchful Fuggers. It was finally decided that when the Indulgence should be promulgated on behalf of rebuilding St. Peter's in Rome, half the proceeds should, by private agreement, go to Albert and the Fuggers. To this Indulgence were attached four privileges: "The plenary remission of all sins; a confession letter allowing the penitent to choose his Confessor; the participation in the Metits of the Saints; and last for the souls in purgatory." Albert's own instructions to his subcommissary were carefully worded to include the phrase *corde contritus et ore confessus*, i.e., they presupposed contrition and confession. But the pardoners went discreetly to work. The literature of ecclesiastical rebuilding schemes rarely attains the higher levels of enlightenment, but the sermons of John Tetzel (1470-1519), the Dominican charged to dispose of Indulgences in Saxony and Brandenburg, touched new depths. The Indulgence procession moved from town to town with the devout furor of a modern ecclesiastical exhibition. "The Bull was borne on a satin or gold-embroidered cushion, and all the priests and monks, the town council, schoolmasters, scholars, men, women, maidens and children went out to meet him with banners and tapers, with songs and processions. Then all the bells were rung, all the organs played . . . a Red Cross was erected in the midst of the church, and the Pope's banner displayed."

For Luther, it was no new concern, for he had already spoken out publicly on the subject. God's forgiveness could not be bought or sold. On the other hand, for Luther to protest against Albert of Mainz was to invite the public suspicion that he was but the tool of the jealous interests of the House of Wettin. But the Indulgence controversy caused a good deal of comment, and in public and private Luther had been asked for his advice. Once again, he sat down and wrote a series of theses. He wrote fluently, for he had a gift for this kind of writing, and if there were some points on which he was uncertain, and which went beyond his own definite conviction, these were, after all, Latin disputations which traditionally had a good deal of license. It was Luther's intention to investigate the truth through academic disputation. Rather than put up a student to argue these theses as was normal procedure, Luther elected to stand himself and argue out the truth from his own theses.

However, copies of Luther's theses fell into the hands of Albert of Mainz, which he forwarded on to Rome, with the request that Luther be restrained. In February 1518, orders to this effect were handed to Gabriel della Volta, Promagistrate of the Augustinian Order, and the command was transmitted to John Staupitz. The Dominicans were up in arms over Luther's actions. At their Saxon Chapter in January 1518, Tetzel propounded a series of counter-theses and formally charged Luther at Rome on suspicion of heresy. The German Dominicans were soon boasting that Luther would be burned, and there must have been many at the time who saw in the controversy just one more squabble among the always quarreling religious. Tetzel sent 800 copies of his theses to Wittenberg, where the adventurous "peddler of religious books," was roughly manhandled by the students who made a bonfire of the documents, winning a reprimand from the authorities since the tumult could hardly have helped Luther at this delicate juncture.

Alarmed though Luther's fellow Augustinians might be, they had no intention of throwing him to the Dominicans. So Luther set out in April 1518 for the Chapter at Heidelberg, despite alarming rumors of impending danger, and provided with letters of credence of such high testimony that one official exclaimed, "By God, that's a fine passport they've given you!"

When the Chapter opened far from being in disgrace, the occasion became an unexpected triumph for Luther. He was relieved of the post of District Vicar, which was given to his friend Lang, but this was a wise tactical move and it must, under the circumstances, have been a welcomed relief. Luther himself presided at a full-dress theological disputation where the Indulgences were forgotten, and once more the battle raged around the Aristotelian Nominalists and the new antidote offered by Wittenberg.

The debate was lively and there was some opposition, but it was among the younger men that Luther made his conquests that day. The Reformation, like every other movement, cut through the generations, and the older men were not much impressed.

Luther got a lift back home, traveling part of the way with his old teacher, Usingen. As the wagon jolted and rumbled along, Luther poured out his soul with eager fire, but the time and the place were not timely for a seminar, and he left the old man glum and silent, and a little dazed. To be cooped up with Martin Luther at close quarters in this exuberant stage of his career must have been a most trying experience.

In May, Luther sent a copy of his Resolutions with a letter of humble appeal to Pope Leo X. In this dispatch Luther tried to temper his own forthright vehemence to the diplomacy of more tactful friends. In the same month, the Dominican Chapter met in Rome, and Tetzel was awarded a doctorate (a year later, discredited and disgraced, he was to die in Leipzig). Matters now took a more serious turn in Luther's case. In March he had preached a fiery sermon about the notorious abuse of the power of excommunication for trivial offenses. Two Domincans, who probably attended the service for devious purposes, extracted articles from the sermon, exaggerated them and dispatched them with some even more dubious gossip to Rome. In the meantime they had enlisted the interest of the Emperor, through Cardinal Cajetan. On the ground of this spurious information, Luther was declared to be a notorious heretic, and the formal citation to Rome was interrupted by a new order to Cajetan to arrest Luther and to order the Augustinian authorities in Germany to carry out the arrest.

Discussion Questions

PART 1 — THE EARLY YEARS

1. Discuss what the religious atmosphere was and what religious controversies were prevalent during Martin Luther's day.

2. What, if any, influence did Luther's father have with his son's joining the monastic life?

3. Do you ever feel alienated from God and long for a reconciliation? How do you go about this reconciliation?

4. Discuss the feeling of unworthiness that Luther felt. Do you ever feel the same way? Do you run to the church to seek escape from this feeling? Is this the right approach?

5. It has been said that Lutheranism was born to teach. Why do you or don't you believe this is so?

6. Why is it that Luther did not find inner peace in the monastic life?

7. What was the purpose of academic disputation during Luther's time? Would it be appropriate in modern times?

8. Discuss the Doctrine of Indulgences, which caused Luther dismay.

9. Discuss how persons can be sure that their sins are forgiven. Is this remission found in Scripture. Where?

10. Central to the Augsburg Confession is a concern that the church be shaped by the gospel — the good news of the life, death and resurrection of Jesus Christ. What is meant by being shaped by the gospel?

PART 2

Controversy With
Rome And The
Diet Of Worms

Exsurge Domine — "Arise, Lord! Judge your cause . . . A wild Boar is destroying your vineyard . . ." With this exhortation Martin Luther sealed his fate. Rome had spoken. Luther had answered. Now it was time for the Emperor to act. Pressured by the Senior Elector, Frederick the Wise, to give Luther a hearing before condemnation, Charles summoned the reformer under safe-conduct to Worms.

The Luther Memorial in the city of Worms is a magnificent reminder of the Reformer. An enormous Luther (3.2 meters high) stands notably in the center, gazing skyward with heroic intensity, cuddling an enormous Bible. And, there, among the number of lesser, stands the figure (2.8 meters high) of the Elector Frederick the Wise.

The Elector Frederick earned his place on the memorial. He could have had little sympathy with Luther's theological protest against Indulgences. But he had a lively concern for his university and respect for all he had heard about Martin Luther. He had enough patriotism to be unwilling to sacrifice Luther as a ruse to the cruel mercies of the Curia. But it is well to be remembered that at almost anytime, had he so willed, the Elector could have ended the career of Martin Luther, and that it was due to him that Wittenberg remained for Luther the strangely calm center of the cyclonic storm which raged all about him. It is indeed a strange situation that Luther was spared by a process of politics (the Pope needed Frederick's goodwill) and "back-scratching."

Luther's defiance at Worms is well known. Most prominent of the actions at Worms were the four momentous interviews with Cardinal Cajetan. If Luther had been so simple as to suppose authority would bandy words with him, he was soon disillusioned. The Cardinal told him he was to do three things: repent and revoke his errors, promise not to teach them again, and refrain from all future mischievous activities.

Affairs reached an impasse which only action could break. On October 16, Staupitz and Link judged matters to be so dangerous as to demand their own hasty withdrawal from the city. Students were becoming hostile and some physical injuries had occurred. Luther wrote a formal appeal to the Pope and a long letter to Cardinal Cajetan.

As hours and days slipped away in ominous silence, Luther's friends became alarmed, and finally, in view of a persistent rumor that Martin was to be seized and sent in chains to Rome, they panicked. Luther was suddenly bundled out through the postern gate, ill-clad and ill-mounted, he rode until forced to stop from exhaustion. A letter he received a few days later confirmed the fact that he had gotten away just in time.

Two important figures emerged in 1519, the Papal Agent, Charles von Miltitz, and Dr. Johann Eck, the theologian from Ingolstadt. Miltitz was of the florid 16th century type, an Italianate German with enormous self-confidence, always planning diplomatic gestures on a grand scale which deceived nobody more than himself. Eck, on the other hand, was a theologian with prodigious memory, steeped in scholasticism, skilled in disputation. He was also vain, loud-mouthed, violent, and a heavy drinker, who according to an unamiable account looked very much like a butcher.

Miltitz came replenished with polite bribes which ranged from dispensations for Frederick's illegitimate children to the great compliment of the Golden Rose for devout parents. Miltitz promised to arrange for a more impartial arbitrator in this Luther affair, the Archbishop of Salzburg, perhaps, or His Grace of Trier. Eck, on the other hand, had struck up a friendship with Luther in 1517 and Luther was deeply hurt and angered when Eck circulated among his friends a slashing attack on Martin Luther's theses.

During the confrontation, Johann Eck drew Martin Luther into a grueling disputation (something Luther had been hoping for) which took place at Leipzig at the beginning of July 1519 and lasted for 11 days. Before the hostile Duke George's Court, the huge-voiced Eck got Luther to deny the divine origin of the papal supremacy and to assert that the heretical John Hus was correct in his statement about abuses in church practice also that many of John Hus and the Hussites beliefs are truly Christian and evangelical and the council that condemned him was in error.

There was a moment of silence, and then an uproar above which could be heard Duke George's disgusted, "Gad, Sir, that's the plague!" For Luther had, in fact, moved beyond discussion of papal power: he had called into question the authority of the great German Council which had so proudly achieved a reunion of the broken Christian world. Eck pressed home his advantage, and Luther, trapped, admitted that since their decrees were also of human law, councils may err. The rest was anti-climax. Eck could afford to make confessions about the Indulgence issue now that Luther had made this huge admission.

Branding Luther a heathen, a triumphant Eck went to Rome, helped prepare the Bull *Exsurge Domine*, condemning Luther's "errors," and returned to publish it in German cities.

Like a prizefighter at the bell, Luther leaped to each challenge. He felt "more acted upon than acting." "I cannot control my life," he confessed. "I am driven into the middle of the storm." Asserting, "It was the love of truth that drove me to enter this labyrinth and stir up six hundred Minotaurs." He little realized the explosive power of the anger bottled up since childhood — first directed against his own severe, unapproving father, then against a judgmental Father in heaven. Now he vented it on his Holy Father in the hierarchical church, who he felt had failed to feed the faithful the indispensable Word of God.

In the crucible of confrontation, Luther forged his creed: *sola scriptura, sola gratia, sola fide.* Only through Holy Scriptures, only from God's Grace, only through faith in Christ does the Christian receive salvation.

The clarity of his teaching packaged a hundred years of Europe's religious yearnings into simple hard-hitting concepts that could be pounded home from countless pulpits and printing presses, spreading the Reformation far and wide.

The years 1519-21 saw a prodigious mental activity which drew from Luther a vast, tumultuous flood of ideas, as tracts, treatises, commentaries, polemic, trod on heels of one another, too fast for three printing presses to keep pace. "I hold the sword with one hand, and with the other build the wall, lest should I accomplish neither." It is as though the distinction between wrath and mercy were reflected in his mind, since his writings fall roughly into these two categories. He found he could write for common people in the language which they could understand.

Martin Luther wrote his classic tract, *Of Good Works* (1520), at the request of Spalatin, librarian, secretary and chaplain to the Elector Frederick the Wise. It disproves two common misconceptions, that Luther was not really concerned with morality, and that his doctrine of justification leaves Christian ethics hanging in the air.

Martin Luther demonstrates how Christian behavior derives from the fact that "the first, the highest and most precious of all good works is faith in Christ." Faith for Luther is, as in the New Testament, not one of a long agenda of virtues, but a whole dimension of Christian existence, with hope and love the fountain from which the Christian life must spring. The Christian man moves in two worlds: a world which is hid with Christ in God, and the visible, fallen, tangible world where also God has called and placed him. (This two-world concept was first espoused by St. Augustine and perhaps Luther had studied and taught this idea at Wittenberg University.) Faith is the point where the Christian unites both worlds, and Luther's Doctrine of Temptation *(Anfechtung)* is seen to be the affirmation that the ultimate, unremitting Christian warfare is this good fight of faith, which comes home to the Christian in the real decision of everyday life.

Luther states the Christian does good works "because it is a pleasure to please God, and he serves God purely and for nothing, content that his service pleases God. On the other hand, he who is not at one with God, or who is in a state of doubts, hunts and worries in what he may do enough, and with many works, to move God." So, "Faith must be in all works the master workman, or captain, or they are nothing at all." Thus, faith is evoked when we turn to Christ.

Luther's relations with the Humanists are complex. In Erfurt, their circle was formed after his profession, but its members included some of his former undergraduate friends, and when he took his Plautus and Virgil with him into the monastery he must have had some thought of continuing classical studies. But Luther was primarily a theologian and preacher, not an academic. He was sensible very early in life of a difference between his theological beliefs and the Humanists. Their catchword, the "renaissance of Christ" was alien to his way of thinking.

As Luther moved out into public controversy, the admiration of the Humanists deepened, the more so as they found it difficult to get full information about his then controversial doctrines. Conflagration flared increasingly between Luther and the Papal Nuncio. For a few months it seemed that Martin

Luther, "the hero of the German nation," might fuse the people into a national revival out of which it might find independence and equilibrium of soul. Eck was appointed to bring the Papal Bull to the southern German cities ordering Luther to recant. He was horrified to find how swiftly public opinion was moving to the side of Luther.

In his "address to the Christian nobility of the German nation," Luther urged the abolishing or curtailing of pilgrimages, privately endowed masses, the veneration of the saints, indulgences, festival days and the interdicts. He asserted heretics are to be refuted with arguments, not with fire. Priests should marry or not as they choose. Luther rejected the sacramental system as having no basis in Scripture except for baptism and the eucharist. Next Luther moved on to refute the infallibility of the Pope and claimed that the Pope had no power to establish new Articles of Faith, and that he was not above, but under, the Word of God. He concluded that the Papacy was a human invention of which God knew nothing. All this from the one-time friar who would rather die than show disrespect for the pope.

Finally, Luther's life reached a turning point in his thoughts about the Roman Church. He wrote these final words: "Farewell, unhappy, hopeless, blasphemous Rome! The Wrath of God hath come upon thee, as thou deservest. We have cared for Babylon, and she is not healed: let us leave her, that she may be the habitation of dragons, spectres and witches, and true to her name of Babel, an everlasting confusion, a new pantheon of wickedness." Through all of this the expected Bull of Excommunication did not come from the authority sitting in Rome. Still they hoped to silence this man, but this was impossible.

It was finally decided that Luther should stand before the Diet for a hearing. This maneuvering was both politically and religiously contrived. For if it proved possible to gain a hearing for the heretic before the Diet, instead of following the traditional course of adding the Imperial ban to the papal ban without further ado (in itself an unheard-of innovation in canon and imperial law) then this was due to the general anger in the imperial estates against "Rome's mismanagement" and also to the concern of the nobility at the burning rage of the common peasant, who was not again to be cheated of his hope for general reform. This first Diet of the new emperor was at last to put into force the reforms of the empire and the church, which had for decades been vainly urged and which in the end it had been impossible to discuss seriously with Maximilian.

Few events in German history have been retold more often than the appearance of Martin Luther before the emperor and the empire. The Imperial Diet of Worms in 1521 is of great importance for the history of the German Constitution; all this has long since been forgotten by many, and only the proceedings with Luther have remained alive in the minds of the German people. In front of the full assembly he was challenged to recant his heresies. But he recanted nothing, and instead delivered a courageous confession of his own convictions and beliefs. The last sentence of his oration, "Here I stand, I cannot do otherwise, God help me! Amen," has rightly become the symbolic expression of all that made Martin Luther, with the heroic submission of his will to the demands of faith, so dear to his nation.

The path he was treading led straight to chaos. The whole terrible weight of historical responsibility lay on his soul. Once again an honorable way out seemed to be opened up to the heretic, condemned to death and excommunicate as he was: had not he himself appealed often enough to the Pope? Was there not, after all, a possibility of a settlement? There were times in these days in which he seemed uncertain in himself about the way out of the confusion of political cul-de-sacs in which they tried to trap him. At one time his nerves seemed near the breaking point: he was close to tears. In a state of great excitement he made his confession to the Archbishop of Treves, though what he actually said, of course, is not known. Yet in those hours of darkness and decision there often came to his mind the saying, "you shall not put your trust in princes, nor in the children of men, in whom is no salvation." He declared that he could submit to no judge's decision which was not based on the Word of God. He did not abandon the least part of his teaching.

Today there remain critics who reproach him with this as his most fatal mistake. Indeed, who will deny that these hours of decision were hours which determined the whole course of the German Reformation? In that he rejected all the offers of reconciliation which the estates made, he almost compelled them to abandon him as an obstinate heretic. The bloody Edict of Worms, with its disastrous consequences, was the immediate consequence of his refusal to co-operate: in it the outlawing of the heretic was proclaimed, a penalty was imposed on the reading and publication of his writings, a spiritual censorship was imposed on all German literature and a radical ban on all libelous writings against the Pope.

It was the first step on the way to the later Counter-Reformation. Was it completely inevitable? Could not Luther, with good conscience have left a part of his writings to the judgment of a future council, in the sure knowledge that the Pope would not allow this council to take place for a long time, so that meanwhile he could gain time for the spreading of the Word? But, of course, this is all hindsight. Then for Luther the approval of men was of no importance. His responsibility before God was everything.

The history of the reform councils teaches perfectly clearly what was to be expected from a reform of the church which did not start at the very heart of the matter but which set about cutting out external abuses without having first dealt with the diseased roots. Yet it was to this that Luther would inescapably have been driven step by step, if he had once held out his hand in peace.

But would the offer of the committee have been honorably meant? Even if it was, would the negotiators in the estates have been able to maintain their honorable intention of peace against the obvious intention of the emperor and Pope to destroy him in face of the hesitation of the estates which remained faithful to the old creed?

In any case Martin Luther would not have been himself if he had denied his past at this moment. He left Worms unvanquished in every sense: indeed, as the true victor over all the endeavors of the politicians — 'mad' in the eyes of men, but born along by the proud certainty of an unbending conscience.

Discussion Questions

PART 2 — CONTROVERSY WITH ROME AND THE DIET OF WORMS

1. What do you consider to be the turning point in Martin Luther's religious life.

2. Luther's view of God was as a judgmental heavenly father. Discuss the concept that God is apart and distinct from the world that God has created.

3. Give a general description of God, noting those characteristics without which you would not be willing to call him "God."

4. Do you believe that God cares about human beings? If you do believe that God cares, explain the abundance of so much evil and suffering in the world. Why does God allow it to continue?

5. Discuss how Luther viewed Christian faith, and how this is related to the concept of works according to Luther.

6. Should Luther have accepted the offers of reconciliation offered to him at the Diet of Worms? Why or why not?

7. Luther believed that the church of his day was using "words" in a way that was actually hindering the Living Word from reaching the hearts of the people. Do you believe that this condition is present in some churches today? How and in what form?

8. Could you and would you stand up as Luther did before the Diet to public ridicule, condemnation, persecution and even possible death to defend your faith?

PART 3

Luther's Legacy — The Later Years

Martin Luther died on February 18, 1546, at the age of 62. The world has changed much in the 400-plus years since Luther's day. The concluding section will examine the power of his struggle with reform and the legacy that he has left the Christian community today.

Martin Luther's harsh treatment of the papacy and hierarchial structure in Rome was but another instance of his interpretation of what the church should be about. Luther was living up to a saying of Christ's that he was so fond of quoting: "I have not come to bring peace, but a sword." Indeed, it was no great cause of sorrow that God's Word should cause such a storm in the world, on the contrary, a highly delectable sight.

However, this battle cry of the warrior was not Martin Luther's last word to the German people. At Worms, Luther's life had hung in the balance of Charles' chivalry. Now he was an outlaw, and his life hung on a ruse. On his return from the Diet of Worms, he vanished. Rumors spread that he had been slain. However, high in the Thuringian Forest in a mock abduction, Luther was spirited away to the Wartburg, a castle commanding a ridge over Eisenach. Here, tonsure grown out into unruly dark hair, disguised as a bearded squire — Junker Georg - Luther lived 10 months alone with God and the devil under the protective custody of Frederick the Wise. During this period Luther drove himself hard. He worked at a feverish pace on his New Testament, which he translated from Erasmus' Greek in an incredibly short 11 weeks. He was frustrated, lonely, often sick, anxious as an outlaw. In his 50 letters, he mentions being troubled by evil spirits.

Disquieting news from Wittenberg intruded on Luther's solitude. Reformers were pushing ahead at a reckless pace. "Good Lord!" Luther wrote. "Will our people at Wittenberg give wives even to the monks? They will not push a wife on me!" Frederick sent word that "so many sects arose among them that everybody was at sea and no one knew who was the cook and who was the ladle. But that Luther should not risk his life by returning."

Trusting in "a far higher protection" than the sword, Luther boldly mounted the pulpit in Wittenberg's town church and held forth for a week until he had turned the raging torrent of religious revolt.

How rash to smash images, strip away comforting trappings in a heedless rush. He preached what he wrote from Wartburg Castle in "A Faithful Exhortation for all Christians to Shun Riot and Rebellion:" Public order and inner faith should go hand in hand. "The Bible is our vineyard, and there we should all labor and toil," Luther declared. No Pope, no dogma, rather a priesthood of all believers. The trouble was scrutiny of Scriptures produced as many contradictory interpretations as Luther's writings themselves. He now found himself a check rein on the Reformation he had unleashed.

In 1525, Luther urged moderation on peasants, who had taken his sympathy for their grievances as a call to violence. Subjects must suffer, obey and pray instead, Luther admonished. Luther the arch-conservative, was condemning riots and rebellion as always wrong, and was backing secular authority as long as it preserved divine law and order. Luther found it easier to make a revolution than to consolidate one, is the point here.

The decade from 1521 to 1530 was the politically formative period of the Reformation. The beginning was at the Diet of Worms, the conclusion was at Augsburg. But this period in history involves more than just the Reformation, and the Reformation involves more than Martin Luther. When then does the figure of this man tower so prominently in the foreground?

One reason is that Luther was the initiator of the great work. This distinguishes him above the significant men with whom the 16th century was blessed. It is true that although Ulrich Zwingli won his insights without Luther, he later on was quite open to his influences, without fully accepting Luther's position. Others, like Bucer, Blaurer, Bugenhagen, cannot even be imagined without Luther. This applies even to Melanchthon, by far the most excellent mind of the Reformation and Luther's cherished friend, and to John Calvin, whose lofty systematizing and organizational ability advanced the work of the Reformation into areas which Luther would never have reached. Not one of these men regarded himself as anything but a student of Martin Luther.

It is immediately evident that Luther was neither merely a thinker nor an organizer. His life was the very battleground on which the fundamental issues of the Reformation were fought through to their ultimate end. The very things which he suffered through, prayed through, struggled through and achieved in faith, were the realization of the goals toward which the Humanists and Calvin, the great organizer, aspired and labored. In short, Luther's struggle for his faith had indirect significance. He had neither a philosophical program nor world-spanning organizational plans. He was simply himself, went his own way, and fought to its conclusion the demands of faith. It is for this reason that he is so personal, that his labors cannot be appreciated if detached from his personal life, and why he stands before us with greater vitality and immediacy than the systematizers and organizers. Personal directness was Luther's contribution in the course of history.

The view of Luther, as stated earlier, as the heroic warrior is completely wrong if heroism is interpreted in the shallow sense of the latter part of the 19th century; Luther was not a "hero" in this bourgeois sense. His exemplary and vicarious significance lies in the fact that in his search for God he wrestled with death and the devil. That his personal wrestling extended beyond him and took on a universal significance encompassing all the powers of the historical world and ultimately altering the foundations of Europe, was not deliberately planned by him. These things happened because he was an instrument in the hands of God.

The Luther who died at Eisleben, almost 25 years after the Diet of Worms, was no longer the popular hero and the widely esteemed focal point of historic decisions. One could easily get the impression that much work-a-day drabness surrounded his person. He had aged, had gained weight, and had been plagued by many physical ailments. The world in which he had to live no longer looked rosy to him. For him, as for everyone, this world had more disappointments in store than hopes. The chapter of the Reformation, which ends with his death seems so completely immersed in the colorless light of resignation, that the world of the church and the spirit in general, yes, to a certain extent, also the world of scholars, has turned away from the picture of the "old Luther" because it was not very appealing.

But that is certainly wrong. A rebuttal to such a viewpoint might best be expressed this way: The historic greatness of the "old Luther" lies in the fact that up to the last day of his life he lived unswervingly on the basis of the insight which he had recovered and taught: God justifies sinners. It is this sober-mindedness which confers a greatness upon his later years.

The same inspired sobermindedness obtained in his plans for the new church order. These have nothing in common with the flaming emotionalism of the "enthusiasts." The very fact that since the extensive church visitation of 1529 he continually stressed the need for religious instruction, proves that he had no illusions about the people with whom he had to deal. He regarded them not as harbingers of the communion of saints, but as illiterates and dullards in need of instruction and preaching. More than once he stated that the orderly instruction of youth bears fruit and vexes the devil. He admonished parents, teachers and magistrates faithfully to fulfill their obligations to the young generations. On the other hand, however, he realized just as clearly that the world would not be transformed in some magical manner just because Christian sermons could be heard in it. He knew that the gospel would be in a continual state of war with Satan until the end of time.

He was certainly not a sophomoric schoolmaster who wanted to regulate life down to the most minute detail. He was willing to allow those things to exist and grow which do no harm to the gospel. In fact, we see in him a man who inspires us to remember God's forgiving mercy. In this world there can never be any order which fully and exclusively represents God's holy will. All that is reserved for the world to come and for the present we must be content to live in a world in which God's sun shines upon the just and the unjust. But every person who recognizes his own constant need of forgiveness will also know exactly where we owe one another forbearance and forgiveness.

Nor is it true that in his theology the "old Luther" was not the same as he was at the beginning of his career. His theological position remained unaltered. All his life he promulgated only one theology: the Theology of the Cross. This remained the central content of his testimony, and was expanded by his ever-increasing eschatological expectations. Afflictions continue to be among the most essential signs of the true Christian life, just as persecution and oppression remain the most basic marks of the true church. But these signs are simply proof that the Christian and the church are treading the same path which their Master took before them and for them — the road of suffering. Above and behind all these earthly hardships the great and eternal goal of history rises in light, the day of God toward which all temporal events are on the move.

Nor is it true that in his later years Luther's theological creativity diminished in quantity or quality. It was during the last decade of his life that he gave his greatest and most comprehensive series of lectures, the exposition of the Book of Genesis. Here Luther vigorously proposes some of his most essential theological concepts. During his last years his theology and his Christian life were fused into a unity. The vigorous "yes" with which Luther, even in the hour of death, subscribed to his entire theological labors, and completely dominated his Christian life as well. He lived by God's justification of the sinner. This is the very reason why the aging Luther was so untheatrical. It is true that he had very exact ideas about his place in history, and at times he expressed these with utmost candor. But to the end he assumed no pose.

And not least of all, it must be remembered that to the very last Martin Luther remained undaunted. It would have been perfectly normal if, under the duress of bodily afflictions and the diverse threats to his life's work, he had fallen prey to a mood of fatal resignation. But on numerous occasions he expressed the conviction that in the last analysis the enemies of the gospel would be unable to accomplish anything — for "he who is with us is greater than he who is in the world. Christ is mightier than Satan."

On the table of Luther's lodging in Eisleben, a note was found which he had written on the day of his death. It is the last written statement that has come down to us from him. It reveals his profound admiration for Virgil and the writers of antiquity. "Nobody can understand Virgil in his *Bucolics* (Shepherd Poems), unless he has been a shepherd for five years. Nobody can understand Virgil in his *Georgics* (Songs of the Country), unless he has been a plowman for five years. Nobody can understand Cicero in his *Epistles*, unless he has lived for 25 years in a large commonwealth. Let no one think he has sufficiently grasped the Holy Scriptures unless he has governed the church for a hundred years with prophets like Elijah and Elisha, John the Baptist, Christ and the apostles. Don't venture on this divine Aeneid, but rather bow low in reverence before its footprints! We are beggars! That is true."

This declaration stands, to be sure, in direct contrast to the posture of self-assurance assumed by so-called modern man. More than two centuries of the most recent history of thought have endeavored to proclaim and give reality to the theme of man's self-glorification.

Today no one any longer doubts that this attempted rebellion on the part of man has failed. The individual, who had made himself the measure of all things, has now become unsure of himself. He has become homeless in the very same cosmos which he wanted to control by his own powers, without God or ties to a world beyond. We are beggars, that is true, but ultimately the importance lies not in the fact that we are beggars, for rising majestically behind Luther's last word is the faith in God who is the hope of the lowly, the consolation of the sinners, the life of the dying, and who will fill the empty hands of the beggars.

The final chapter in the history of the Reformation has not yet been written. Not only is it being written in our time, we are helping to write it. This does not mean that it is our job to start a new church for our times. If we want to catch the real meaning of the Reformation for us in our time, then we must know what it was in Luther's time. As redeem may mean to buy back the watch you owned before, and renew may mean to make your old car like it was when new, so Reformation means to restore the church to what God intended it to be.

Thus we can reach the conclusion and arrive at the answer to our initial question: Martin Luther: heretic or reformer? Reformer — though he is long gone from the scene, his legacy lives on daily in our Christian community.

Discussion Questions

PART 3 — LUTHER'S LEGACY — LUTHER'S LATER YEARS

1. Discuss what Martin Luther thought should be the main concern of the church. Does this differ from contemporary thought?

2. Discuss the use of and justification for violence. Is there ever a time when it is justified? If so when and for what reason?

3. God, in Jesus, admonished us to love our neighbor. Was this consistent with what Luther initiated?

4. Discuss the statement, "There can never be any order which fully and exclusively represents God's holy will." Do you accept this statement as true? If not, why not?

5. Do you believe that Luther accomplished what he set out to do? If so what?

6. Was the Reformation successful? How so?

7. What do you think Luther meant when he said, "We are beggars, that is true."?

8. Discuss and explain the statement, "We are justified by grace through faith." What do we mean by grace?

9. What did Luther believe hinders us from hearing the Living Word?

10. What did Luther mean by the "Theology of the Cross" as opposed to the "Theology of Glory?" Explain and discuss each.

Works Cited

Atkinson, James, *The Trial of Luther,* New York. Stein & Day Publishers, 1971.

Edwards, Mark U. Jr., *Luther's Last Battles: Politics and Polemics,* Ithaca, N.Y., Cornell University Press, 1983.

Jacobs, H.E., *Works of Martin Luther,* (edited), Philadelphia, Holman & Castle Press, 1932.

Luther, Martin, *The Small Catechism,* (translation), Minneapolis, Augsburg Publishing House, 1968. (1531 original writing)

Meuser, Fred W. and Stanley D. Schneider, *Interpreting Luther's Legacy,* (edited), Minneapolis, Augsburg Publishing House, 1969.

Porter, J.M., *Luther's Selected Political Writings,* (edited), Philadelphia, Fortress Press, 1974.

Rupp, Gordon, *Luther's Progress To The Diet of Worms,* New York, Harper & Row Publishing, 1964.

Rupp, Gordon and Benjamin Drewery, *Documents of History: Martin Luther,* (edited), New York, St. Martin's Press, 1970.

Smith, Preserved *The Life and Letters of Martin Luther,* (edited), Murray, 1911.

Tappert, Theodore G., *The Book of Concord: The Confessions of the Evangelical Lutheran Church,* (translation), Philadelphia, Fortress Press, 1959.

Van Loewenich, Walter, *Luther's Theology of The Cross,* translated by J.A. Bouman, Minneapolis, Augsburg Publishing House, 1976.